KU-165-472

easy meals

Sizzling Dishes

p

This is a Parragon Book
First printed in 2001

Parragon
Queen Street House
4 Queen Street
Bath BA1 1HE
United Kingdom

ISBN: 0-75255-338-0

Printed in Spain

Produced by The Bridgewater Book Company Ltd, Lewes, East Sussex

Acknowledgements
Creative Director Terry Jeavons
Art Director Sarah Howerd
Editorial Director Fiona Biggs
Senior Editor Mark Truman
Editorial Assistants Tom Kitch
Page Make-up Chris Akroyd

NOTES FOR THE READER

- This book uses both metric and imperial measurements. Follow the same units of measurement throughout; do not mix metric and imperial.
- All spoon measurements are level: teaspoons are assumed to be 5 ml, and tablespoons are assumed to be 15 ml.
- Unless otherwise stated, milk is assumed to be full-fat, eggs and individual vegetables such as potatoes are medium-sized, and pepper is freshly ground black pepper.
- Recipes using raw or very lightly cooked eggs should be avoided by infants, the elderly, pregnant women, convalescents, and anyone suffering from an illness.
- Optional ingredients, variations, and serving suggestions have not been included in the calculations.
- The times given are an approximate guide only. Preparation times differ according to the techniques used by different people and the cooking times vary as a result of the type of oven used.

Contents

Introduction

If your busy life-style leaves you with little spare time for cooking, but you are finding your usual recipes for fast food rather bland and boring, the recipes in this book will be a revelation. Your senses will really sit up and take notice when you present them with these sizzling hot and spicy dishes, bursting with mouthwatering flavours and enticing aromas.

The recipes have been specifically selected because they are easy to prepare and cook, so now even your mid-week meals can be exciting and different. Many of the ingredients can be kept on hand in the storecupboard; all you need to do is add fresh fish or meat and vegetables to create something quite out-of-the-ordinary. The dishes are gathered from a variety of cultures around the world, including Thai, Mexican, and Chinese, and they reflect today's changing attitudes to eating: less heavy and

guide to recipe key	
easy	Recipes are graded as follows: 1 pea = easy; 2 peas = very easy; 3 peas = extremely easy.
serves 4	Most of the recipes in this book serve four people. Simply halve the ingredients to serve two, taking care not to mix imperial and metric measurements.
15 minutes	Preparation time. Where recipes include marinating, soaking, standing, or chilling, times for these are listed separately: eg, 15 minutes, plus 30 minutes to marinate.
15 minutes	Cooking time. Cooking times do not include the cooking of rice or noodles served with the main dishes.

conventional, more adventurous and fun. Many of the dishes are quickly stir-fried or are grilled, so they are even ideal for weight-watchers and the health-conscious.

And if you enjoy entertaining but find yourself with little time to prepare lavish meals, try a simple menu such as Lemon Grass Chicken Skewers followed by Thai-spiced Salmon, with an Exotic Fruit Salad for dessert. It looks and tastes impressive and takes little time to assemble and cook, enabling you to unwind with your guests on any day of the week.

Fish Tacos, page 60

Soups, Starters & Light Dishes

This first part of the book is full of ideas for soups and other first-course dishes which would also make a light lunch or a one-dish supper. Chicken, Avocado & Chipotle Soup includes all the classic ingredients of Mexican cooking. Hot and Sour Noodles is a snack served all day long from market stalls in Thailand. Red Rice Salad with Hot Dressing is just one spicy alternative for vegetarians who like a sizzle to their suppers.

Parsnip Soup with Ginger & Orange

INGREDIENTS

2 tsp olive oil
1 large onion, chopped
1 large leek, sliced
800 g/1 lb 12 oz parsnips, sliced
2 carrots, sliced thinly
4 tbsp grated peeled fresh ginger
2–3 garlic cloves, chopped finely
grated rind of ½ orange
1.7 litres/3 pints water
salt and pepper
250 ml/9 fl oz orange juice
snipped chives or slivers of spring onion, to garnish

very easy

serves 6

15 minutes

50 minutes

VARIATION
The soup may be made using equal amounts (450 g/1 lb each) of carrots and parsnips.

❶ Heat the olive oil in a large saucepan over a medium heat. Add the onion and leek and cook for about 5 minutes, stirring occasionally, until softened.

❷ Add the parsnips, carrots, ginger, garlic, grated orange rind, water, and a large pinch of salt. Reduce the heat, cover and simmer for about 40 minutes, stirring occasionally, until the vegetables are very soft.

❸ Allow the soup to cool slightly, then transfer to a blender or a food processor and blend until smooth, working in batches if necessary. (If using a food processor, strain off the cooking liquid and reserve. Purée the soup solids with enough cooking liquid to moisten them, then combine with the remaining liquid.)

❹ Return the soup to the saucepan and stir in the orange juice. If you prefer a thinner consistency, add a little water or more orange juice. Taste and, if necessary, adjust the seasoning with salt and pepper.

❺ Simmer the soup for about 10 minutes to heat it through. Ladle into warm bowls, garnish with chives or slivers of spring onion, and serve.

Spicy Lamb Soup with Chickpeas & Courgettes

INGREDIENTS

1–2 tbsp olive oil
450 g/1 lb lean boneless lamb, such as shoulder or neck fillet, trimmed of fat and cut into 1 cm/½ inch cubes
1 onion, chopped finely
2–3 garlic cloves, crushed
1.3 litres/2¼ pints water
400 g/14 oz canned chopped tomatoes
1 bay leaf
½ tsp dried thyme
½ tsp dried oregano
⅛ tsp ground cinnamon
¼ tsp ground cumin
¼ tsp ground turmeric
1 tsp harissa, or larger quantity to taste
400 g/14 oz canned chickpeas, rinsed and drained
1 carrot, diced
1 potato, diced
1 courgette, quartered lengthways and sliced
100 g/3½ oz fresh or defrosted frozen green peas
chopped fresh mint or coriander, to garnish

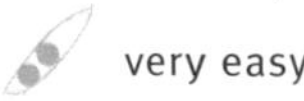

very easy

serves 4–5

20 minutes

1 hour 45 minutes

1 Heat the oil in a large saucepan or cast-iron casserole over a medium-high heat. Add the lamb, in batches if necessary to avoid crowding the pan, and fry until evenly browned on all sides, adding a little more oil if needed. Remove the meat with a slotted spoon when browned.

2 Reduce the heat and add the onion and garlic to the pan. Cook, stirring frequently, for 1–2 minutes.

3 Add the water and return all the meat to the pan. Bring to the boil and skim off any foam that rises to the surface. Reduce the heat and stir in the tomatoes and their juices, the bay leaf, thyme, oregano, cinnamon, cumin, turmeric and harissa. Simmer for about 1 hour, or until the meat is very tender. Discard the bay leaf.

4 Stir in the chickpeas, carrot and potato, and simmer for 15 minutes. Add the courgette and peas and continue simmering the soup for 15–20 minutes, or until all the vegetables are tender.

5 Adjust the seasoning, adding more harissa if required. Ladle the soup into warm bowls, and garnish with mint or coriander before serving.

Spicy Gazpacho

INGREDIENTS

1 cucumber
2 green peppers
½ fresh hot chilli
6 ripe, tasty tomatoes
½ onion, chopped finely
3–4 garlic cloves, chopped
4 tbsp extra-virgin olive oil
½–¾ tsp ground cumin
2 tsp sherry vinegar, or a combination of balsamic vinegar and wine vinegar
4 tbsp chopped fresh coriander
2 tbsp chopped fresh parsley
450 ml/16 fl oz tomato juice, or canned, chopped tomatoes
salt and pepper
ice cubes, to serve

 very easy

 serves 4–6

 30 minutes, plus a few hours to chill

 0 minutes

COOK'S TIP
Freeze tomato juice in an ice cube tray and use the cubes as a delicious alternative to plain ice cubes.

❶ Peel the cucumber, cut it in half lengthways, then cut it into quarters. Remove the seeds with a teaspoon and dice the flesh. Cut the peppers in half, remove the cores and seeds, then dice the flesh. Deseed and chop the chilli.

❷ If you prefer to skin the tomatoes, place in a heatproof bowl, pour boiling water over to cover them, and leave them to stand for 30 seconds. Drain and plunge into cold water. The skins will then slide off easily. Cut the tomatoes in half, deseed if you prefer, then chop the flesh.

❸ Combine half the cucumber, peppers, tomatoes and onion in a blender or a food processor with all the chilli, garlic, olive oil, cumin, vinegar, coriander and parsley. Process with a sufficient quantity of the tomato juice to make a smooth purée.

❹ Pour the puréed soup into a bowl and stir in the remaining green peppers, cucumber, tomatoes and onion, and tomato juice. Season with salt and pepper to taste, then cover and chill in the refrigerator for a few hours.

❺ To serve, stir, ladle the gazpacho into soup bowls and add 1–2 ice cubes to each portion.

Chicken, Avocado & Chipotle Soup

INGREDIENTS

1.5 litres/2 ¾ pints chicken stock
2–3 garlic cloves
1–2 chipotle chillies
1 avocado
lime or lemon juice, for tossing
3–5 spring onions, sliced thinly
350–400 g/12–14 oz cooked chicken breast meat, torn, shredded, or cut into thin strips
2 tbsp chopped fresh coriander

TO SERVE
1 lime, cut into wedges
handful of tortilla chips

 extremely easy

 serves 4

 15 minutes

 20 minutes

COOK'S TIP

Chipotle chillies are smoked, dried jalapeño chillies. They are very hot. If possible, use chipotles canned in adobo marinade for this recipe.

❶ Chop the garlic cloves finely, cut the chipotle chillies into very thin strips, and place them in a pan with the chicken stock, and bring to the boil.

❷ Meanwhile, cut the avocado in half around the stone. Twist apart, then remove the stone with a knife. Peel off the skin carefully, dice the flesh, and toss in lime or lemon juice to prevent discoloration.

❸ Place the spring onions, chicken, avocado and coriander in the base of four soup bowls or in a large serving bowl.

❹ Ladle the hot stock into the bowls, and serve with lime wedges and a handful of tortilla chips.

Hot & Sour Soup

INGREDIENTS

350 g/12 oz whole raw or cooked tiger prawns in their shells
1 tbsp vegetable oil
1 lemon grass stalk, chopped roughly
2 kaffir lime leaves, shredded
1 green chilli, deseeded and chopped
1.3 litres/$2\frac{1}{4}$ pints chicken or fish stock
1 lime
1 tbsp Thai fish sauce
salt and pepper
1 red bird's-eye chilli, deseeded and sliced
1 spring onion, sliced
1 tbsp chopped coriander, to garnish

very easy

serves 4

20 minutes

30 minutes

COOK'S TIP
To devein the tiger prawns, remove the shells. Cut a slit along the back of each prawn and remove the fine black vein that runs along the length of the back. Wipe the prawn with kitchen paper.

❶ Peel and devein the tiger prawns, then cover and chill until needed. Reserve the shells.

❷ Heat the oil in a large pan and stir-fry the prawn shells for 3–4 minutes until they turn pink. Add the lemon grass, lime leaves, green chilli and stock. Pare a strip of zest from the lime and add to the pan.

❸ Bring to the boil, then lower the heat, cover, and simmer for about 20 minutes.

❹ Strain the liquid and pour it back into the pan. Squeeze the juice from the lime and add to the pan with the fish sauce and salt and pepper to taste.

❺ Return to the boil, then lower the heat, add the tiger prawns, and simmer for 2–3 minutes.

❻ Add the thinly sliced red bird's-eye chilli and spring onion. Sprinkle with coriander and serve.

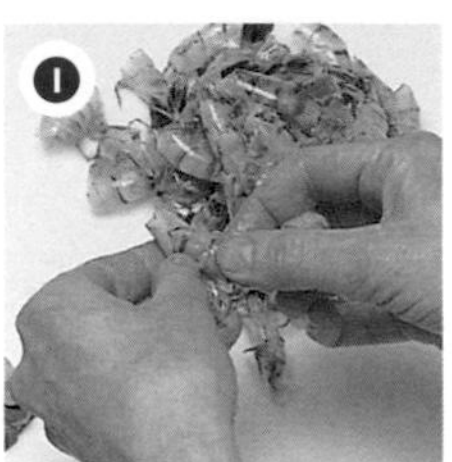
❶

❷

❺

Roasted Spare Ribs with Honey & Soy Sauce

INGREDIENTS

1 kg/2 lb 4 oz Chinese-style spare ribs
½ lemon
½ small orange
2.5 cm/1 inch piece fresh ginger, peeled
2 garlic cloves, peeled
1 small onion, chopped
2 tbsp soy sauce
2 tbsp rice wine
½ tsp Thai 7-spice powder
2 tbsp honey
1 tbsp sesame oil

very easy

serves 4

15 minutes

1 hour
10 minutes

❶ Place the ribs in a wide roasting tin, cover loosely with foil, and cook in an oven preheated to 180°C/350°F/Gas Mark 4 for 30 minutes.

❷ Meanwhile, remove any seeds from the lemon and orange and place the fruit in a food processor with the ginger, garlic, onion, soy sauce, rice wine, 7-spice powder, honey and sesame oil. Process until smooth.

❸ Pour off any fat from the spare ribs, then spoon the puréed mixture over them. Toss the ribs to coat evenly.

❹ Return the ribs to the oven at 200°C/400°F/Gas Mark 6 and roast for about 40 minutes, turning and basting them occasionally, or until golden brown. Serve hot.

COOK'S TIP
If you do not have a food processor, grate the rind and squeeze the juice from the citrus fruits, grate the ginger, crush the garlic, and chop the onion finely. Mix together with the remaining ingredients.

Lemon Grass Chicken Skewers

INGREDIENTS

2 long or 4 short lemon grass stalks
2 large boneless, skinless chicken breasts, about 400 g/ 14 oz in total
1 small egg white
1 carrot, grated finely
1 small red chilli, deseeded and chopped
2 tbsp chopped fresh garlic chives
2 tbsp chopped fresh coriander
salt and pepper
1 tbsp sunflower oil
coriander and slices of lime, to garnish

 very easy

 serves 4

 15 minutes, plus 15 minutes to chill

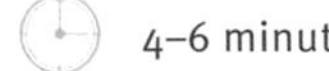 4–6 minutes

COOK'S TIP
If you cannot buy whole lemon grass stalks, use wooden or bamboo skewers instead, and add ½ teaspoon ground lemon grass to the mixture with the other flavourings.

1. If the lemon grass stalks are long, cut them in half across the middle to make 4 short lengths. Cut each stalk in half lengthways, so you have 8 sticks.

2. Roughly chop the chicken pieces and place them in a food processor with the egg white. Process to a smooth paste, then add the carrot, chilli, chives, coriander and salt and pepper. Process for a few seconds to mix well.

3. Chill the mixture in the refrigerator for about 15 minutes. Divide into 8 equal portions, then use your hands to shape each portion round one of the skewers of lemon grass.

4. Brush the skewers with sunflower oil and grill under a preheated medium–hot grill for 4–6 minutes, turning them occasionally, until golden brown and cooked thoroughly. Alternatively, grill over medium-hot coals.

5. Serve hot, with coriander and slices of lime to garnish.

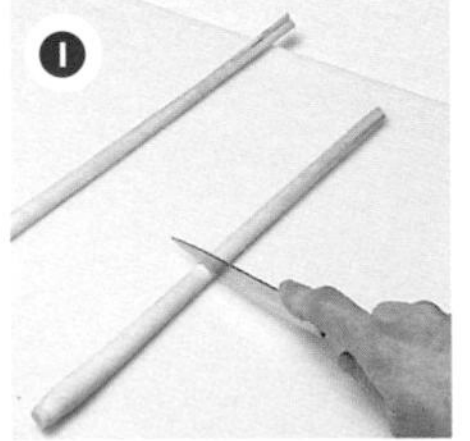
1

3

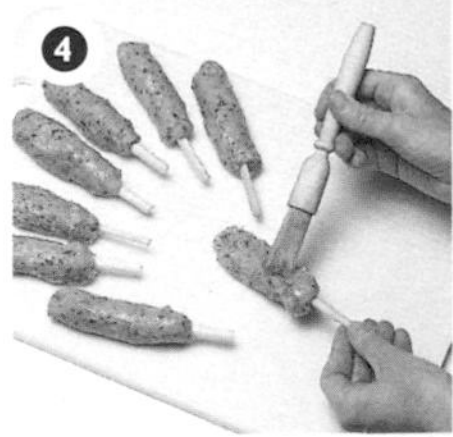
4

Beef Satay with Peanut Sauce

INGREDIENTS

500 g/1 lb 2 oz beef fillet
2 garlic cloves, crushed
8 mm/¾ inch piece fresh ginger, grated finely
1 tbsp soft brown sugar
1 tbsp dark soy sauce
1 tbsp lime juice
2 tsp sesame oil
1 tsp ground coriander
1 tsp turmeric
½ tsp chilli powder
crisp salad, to serve

PEANUT SAUCE
8 tbsp crunchy peanut butter
½ small onion, grated
375 ml/13 fl oz coconut milk
2 tsp soft light brown sugar
½ tsp chilli powder
1 tbsp dark soy sauce

 very easy

 serves 4

 10 minutes, plus 2 hours to marinate

 3–5 minutes

COOK'S TIP
Soak the skewers in cold water for about 20 minutes before threading the meat onto them to reduce the risk of them burning on the grill.

1. Cut the beef into 1 cm/½ inch cubes.

2. Place the beef cubes in a large bowl and add the garlic, ginger, sugar, soy sauce, lime juice, sesame oil, ground coriander, turmeric and chilli powder. Mix well to coat the pieces of meat evenly. Cover and leave to marinate in the refrigerator for at least 2 hours, or overnight.

3. To make the peanut sauce, place all the ingredients in a saucepan and stir over a medium heat until they boil. Remove from the heat and keep warm.

4. Thread the beef cubes onto bamboo skewers. Grill under a preheated grill for 3–5 minutes, turning often, until golden. Alternatively, barbecue over hot coals. Serve with the peanut sauce and a crisp salad.

Hot & Sour Noodles

INGREDIENTS

250 g/9 oz dried medium egg noodles
1 tbsp sesame oil
1 tbsp chilli oil
1 garlic clove, crushed
2 spring onions, chopped finely
140 g/5 oz button mushrooms, sliced
200 g/7 oz dried Chinese black mushrooms, soaked, drained and sliced
2 tbsp lime juice
3 tbsp light soy sauce
1 tsp sugar

TO SERVE
shredded Chinese cabbage
2 tbsp chopped coriander
2 tbsp toasted peanuts

 extremely easy

 serves 4

 10 minutes, plus 2 hours to soak

 15 minutes

COOK'S TIP
Thai chilli oil is very hot, so if you want a milder flavour, use vegetable oil to cook and dribble a little chilli oil over the noodles as a seasoning just before serving.

❶ Cook the noodles in a large pan of boiling water for 3–4 minutes, or according to the package directions. Drain well, then toss with the sesame oil and set aside.

❷ Heat the chilli oil in a large wok and quickly stir-fry the garlic, spring onions and button mushrooms until softened.

❸ Add the black mushrooms, lime juice, soy sauce and sugar, and stir-fry until the mushrooms are cooked. Add the noodles and toss to mix. Spoon the mixture over Chinese cabbage, sprinkle with coriander and peanuts, and serve.

Roasted Cheese with Salsa

INGREDIENTS

225 g/8 oz mozzarella, fresh pecorino or Mexican queso Oaxaca
150 ml/5 fl oz tomato salsa
½ onion, chopped finely
8 soft corn tortillas, to serve

extremely easy

serves 4

5 minutes

20 minutes

1. To warm the corn tortillas ready for serving, heat a non-stick frying pan, put in a tortilla, and sprinkle it with a few drops of water as it heats. Wrap it in kitchen foil to keep it warm. Repeat the process with the remaining tortillas.

2. Cut chunks or slabs of the cheese and arrange in a shallow ovenproof dish or in individual dishes.

3. Spoon the salsa over the cheese, covering it, and place in a preheated oven at 200°C/400°F/Gas Mark 6, or under a preheated grill. Cook until the cheese melts and bubbles, lightly browning in spots.

4. Sprinkle with chopped onion to taste, and serve with the warmed tortillas for dipping. Serve the dish immediately, because the melted cheese turns stringy when it is cold and becomes difficult to eat.

COOK'S TIP

Queso Oaxaca is the authentic cheese to use, but mozzarella or pecorino make excellent substitutes as they produce the right effect when melted.

Prawn Satay

INGREDIENTS

12 peeled raw tiger prawns

MARINADE
1 tsp ground coriander
1 tsp ground cumin
2 tbsp light soy sauce
4 tbsp vegetable oil
1 tbsp curry powder
1 tbsp ground turmeric
125 ml/4 fl oz coconut milk
3 tbsp sugar

PEANUT SAUCE
2 tbsp vegetable oil
3 garlic cloves, crushed
1 tbsp red curry paste
125 ml/4 fl oz coconut milk
300 ml/10 fl oz fish or chicken stock
1 tbsp sugar
1 tsp salt
1 tbsp lemon juice
4 tbsp unsalted roasted peanuts, chopped finely
4 tbsp dried breadcrumbs

 very easy

 serves 4

 20 minutes, plus 8 hours to marinate

 15 minutes

❶ Slit the prawns down their backs and remove the black vein, if any. Mix together the marinade ingredients and add the prawns. Stir well, cover and set aside for at least 8 hours or overnight.

❷ To make the peanut sauce, heat the oil in a large frying pan until very hot. Add the garlic and fry until just starting to colour. Add the curry paste and mix together, cooking for an additional 30 seconds. Add the coconut milk, stock, sugar, salt and lemon juice, stirring. Bring to the boil and cook for 1–2 minutes, stirring constantly. Add the peanuts and breadcrumbs. Pour the sauce into a bowl and set aside.

❸ Using 4 skewers, thread 3 prawns onto each. Cook under a preheated grill, or on the barbecue, for 3–4 minutes on each side until just cooked through. Serve immediately with the peanut sauce.

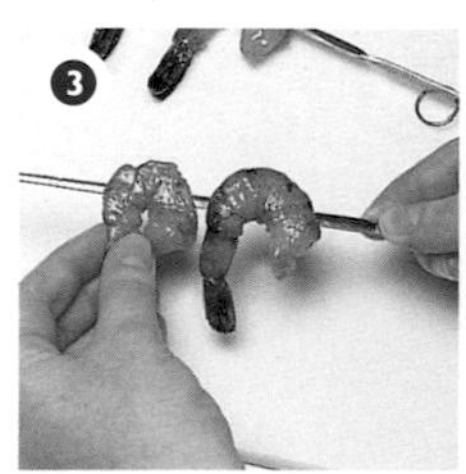

Thai Fish Cakes with Sweet & Sour Chilli Dipping Sauce

INGREDIENTS

450 g/1 lb firm white fish, such as hake, haddock or cod, skinned and chopped roughly
1 tbsp Thai fish sauce
1 tbsp red curry paste
1 kaffir lime leaf, shredded finely
2 tbsp chopped coriander
1 egg
1 tsp brown sugar
large pinch salt
40 g/1½ oz green beans, sliced thinly crossways
vegetable oil, for frying

SWEET & SOUR DIPPING SAUCE
4 tbsp sugar
1 tbsp cold water
3 tbsp white rice vinegar
2 small, hot chillies, chopped finely
1 tbsp fish sauce

 very easy

 serves 4

 15 minutes

 6–8 minutes

❶ To make the fish cakes, put the fish, fish sauce, curry paste, lime leaf, coriander, egg, sugar and salt into the bowl of a food processor. Process until smooth. Scrape into a bowl and stir in the green beans. Set aside.

❷ To make the sweet and sour dipping sauce, put the sugar, water and rice vinegar into a small saucepan and heat gently until the sugar has dissolved. Bring to the boil and simmer for 2 minutes. Remove from the heat and stir in the chillies and fish sauce. Leave to cool.

❸ Pour enough oil into a frying pan to cover the bottom generously, and heat. Divide the fish mixture into 16 little balls. Flatten the balls into patties, and fry in the hot oil for 1–2 minutes each side until golden. Drain on kitchen paper. Serve hot with the dipping sauce.

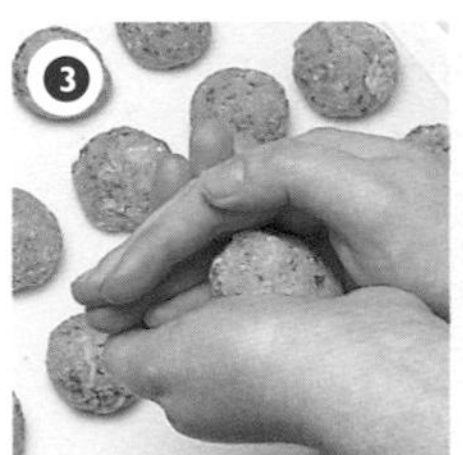

Meat

Beef, lamb, pork and chicken all work well in sizzling, spicy dishes. Red-hot Beef with Cashews can be prepared ahead of a dinner party and finished off quickly when it is time to serve them. The beef is seasoned with intensely flavoured spices, then quickly browned before serving with fried cashews. Chicken & Mango Stir-Fry is a low fat dish with an exciting blend of textures: spicy chicken, crisp vegetables and smooth, sweet mango. It takes just over 30 minutes from preparation to serving. Mumbar, from the Gulf, is a lamb sausage seasoned with exotic spices.

Red-hot Beef with Cashews

INGREDIENTS

500 g/1 lb 2 oz boneless, lean beef sirloin, sliced thinly
1 tsp vegetable oil

MARINADE
1 tbsp sesame seeds
1 garlic clove, chopped
1 tbsp fresh ginger, chopped finely
1 red bird's-eye chilli, chopped
2 tbsp dark soy sauce
1 tsp red curry paste

TO FINISH
1 tsp sesame oil
4 tbsp unsalted cashew nuts
1 spring onion, sliced thickly on the diagonal

very easy

serves 4

20 minutes, plus 2–3 hours to marinate

15 minutes

❶ Cut the beef into strips 1 cm/½ inch wide. Place these in a large, non-metal bowl.

❷ To make the marinade, toast the sesame seeds in a heavy-based pan over a medium heat for 2–3 minutes until golden brown, shaking the pan occasionally.

❸ Place the seeds in a mortar with the garlic, ginger and chilli, and grind with a pestle to a smooth paste. Add the soy sauce and curry paste, and mix well.

❹ Spoon the paste over the beef strips and toss well to coat the meat evenly. Cover and leave to marinate in the refrigerator for 2–3 hours, or overnight.

❺ Heat a heavy frying pan until very hot and brush with vegetable oil. Place the beef strips in it and fry quickly, turning often, until lightly browned. Remove from the heat and spoon onto a hot serving dish, forming a pile.

❻ Heat the sesame oil in a small pan and quickly fry the cashew nuts until they are golden. Add the sliced spring onion and stir-fry for 30 seconds. Sprinkle the mixture over the beef strips, and serve immediately.

❹

❺

❻

Red Lamb Curry

INGREDIENTS

500 g/1 lb 2 oz boneless lean leg of lamb
2 tbsp vegetable oil
1 large onion, sliced
2 garlic cloves, crushed
2 tbsp Thai red curry paste
150 ml/5 fl oz coconut milk
1 tbsp soft light brown sugar
1 large red pepper, deseeded and sliced thickly
125 ml/4 fl oz beef (or lamb) stock
1 tbsp Thai fish sauce
2 tbsp lime juice
225 g/8 oz canned water chestnuts, drained
2 tbsp chopped fresh coriander
2 tbsp chopped fresh basil
salt and pepper
boiled jasmine rice, to serve

very easy

serves 4

20 minutes

45–50 minutes

❶ Trim the meat and cut it into 3 cm/1¼ inch cubes. Heat the oil in a wok over a high heat and stir-fry the onion and garlic for 2–3 minutes to soften. Add the meat cubes and fry quickly until lightly browned.

❷ Stir in the curry paste and cook for a few seconds, then add the coconut milk and sugar and bring to the boil. Reduce the heat and simmer for 15 minutes, stirring occasionally.

❸ Stir in the red pepper, stock, fish sauce and lime juice, cover, and continue simmering for an additional 15 minutes, or until the meat is tender.

❹ Add the water chestnuts, coriander and basil, then adjust the seasoning to taste. Serve with jasmine rice.

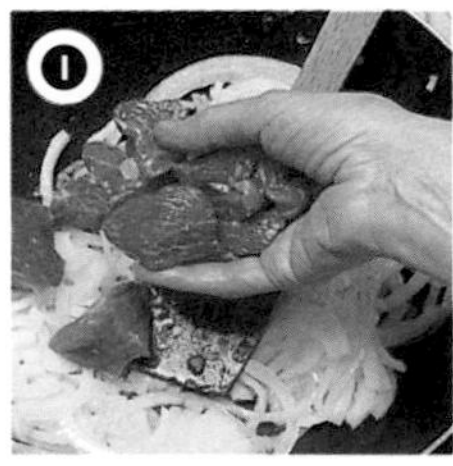

Chicken & Mango Stir-Fry

INGREDIENTS

6 boneless, skinless chicken thighs
2.5 cm/1 inch piece fresh ginger, grated
1 garlic clove, crushed
1 small red chilli, deseeded
1 large red pepper
4 spring onions
150 g/5 oz mangetouts
100 g/3½ oz baby corn
1 large, ripe mango
2 tbsp sunflower oil
1 tbsp light soy sauce
3 tbsp rice wine or sherry
1 tsp sesame oil
salt and pepper
sliced chives, to garnish

❶ Cut the chicken into long, thin strips and place in a bowl. Mix together the ginger, garlic and chilli, then stir into the chicken strips to coat them evenly.

❷ Slice the pepper thinly, cutting diagonally. Trim the spring onions and slice them diagonally, and cut the mangetouts and corn in half diagonally. Peel the mango, remove the stone, and slice the fruit thinly.

❸ Heat the oil in a wok or a large frying pan over a high heat. Add the chicken and stir-fry for 4–5 minutes until it just turns golden brown. Add the peppers and stir-fry over a medium heat for 4–5 minutes to soften. Add the spring onions, corn and mangetouts and stir-fry for 1 more minute.

❹ Mix together the soy sauce, rice wine or sherry and sesame oil. Stir it into the wok. Add the mango and stir gently for 1 minute to heat thoroughly. Adjust the seasoning with salt and pepper to taste, and serve immediately.

 very easy

 serves 4

 20 minutes

 15 minutes

Thai-spiced Coriander Chicken

INGREDIENTS

4 boneless chicken breasts, without skin

MARINADE

2 garlic cloves, peeled
1 fresh green chilli, deseeded
2 cm/¾ inch piece fresh ginger, peeled
4 tbsp chopped fresh coriander
finely grated rind of 1 lime
3 tbsp lime juice
2 tbsp light soy sauce
1 tbsp caster sugar
200 ml/7 fl oz coconut milk

❶ Using a sharp knife, cut 3 deep slashes in the side of each chicken breast. Place the breasts in a single layer, slashed side upward, in a wide, non-metal dish.

❷ Put the garlic, chilli, ginger, coriander, lime rind and juice, soy sauce, caster sugar and coconut milk in a food processor and process until a smooth purée forms.

❸ Spread the purée over both sides of the chicken breasts, coating them evenly. Cover the dish and leave to marinate in the refrigerator for about 1 hour.

❹ Lift the chicken from the marinade, drain off the excess and place in a grill pan. Grill under a preheated grill for 12–15 minutes until cooked thoroughly and evenly.

❺ Meanwhile, put the remaining marinade in a saucepan and bring to the boil. Lower the heat and simmer for several minutes to heat thoroughly. Serve with the chicken breasts.

 very easy

 serves 4

 15 minutes, plus 1 hour to marinate

 15–20 minutes

Duck Breasts with Chilli & Lime

INGREDIENTS

MARINADE
2 garlic cloves, crushed
4 tsp light soft brown sugar
3 tbsp lime juice
1 tbsp soy sauce
1 tsp chilli sauce

4 boneless duck breasts
1 tsp vegetable oil
125 ml/4 fl oz chicken stock
2 tbsp plum jam
salt and pepper

1. Mix together the garlic, sugar, lime juice, and soy and chilli sauces.

2. Using a small sharp knife, cut deep slashes in the skin of the duck to make a diamond pattern. Place the duck breasts in a wide, non-metal dish.

3. Spoon the mixture over the duck breasts, turning well to coat them evenly. Cover the dish with clingfilm and leave to marinate in the refrigerator for at least 3 hours, or overnight.

4. Drain the duck, reserving the marinade. Heat a large, heavy-based pan until very hot and brush with the oil. Add the duck breasts, skin side down, and cook for 4–5 minutes until the skin is browned and crisp. Pour off the excess fat.

5. Turn the duck breasts and cook on the other side for 2–3 minutes to brown. Add the reserved marinade, jam and stock, and simmer for 2 minutes. Adjust the seasoning to taste and serve hot, with the juices spooned over the meat.

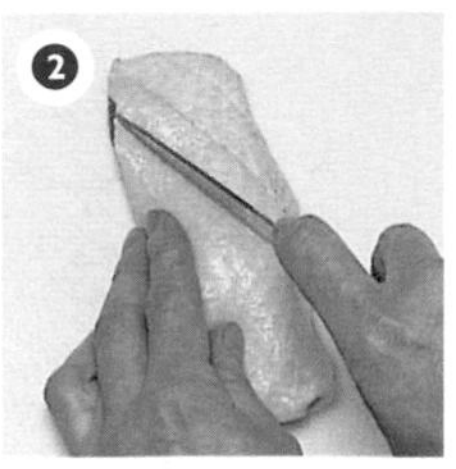

easy

serves 4

15 minutes, plus 3 hours to marinate

10 minutes

Drunken Noodles

INGREDIENTS

175 g/6 oz rice ribbon noodles
2 tbsp vegetable oil
1 garlic clove, crushed
2 small green chillies, chopped
1 small onion, sliced thinly
150 g/5½ oz lean ground pork or chicken
1 small green pepper, deseeded and chopped finely
4 kaffir lime leaves, shredded finely
1 tbsp dark soy sauce
1 tbsp light soy sauce
½ tsp sugar
1 tomato, cut into thin wedges
2 tbsp basil leaves

 very easy

 serves 4

 10 minutes, plus 15 minutes to soak noodles

 5 minutes

COOK'S TIP
Fresh kaffir lime leaves freeze well. If you buy more than you need, tie them in a tightly sealed plastic freezer bag and freeze them for up to a month. They can be used from the freezer.

1. Soak the noodles in hot water for 15 minutes, or according to the package directions. Drain well.

2. Heat the oil in a wok and stir-fry the garlic, chillies and onion for 1 minute. Stir in the pork or chicken and stir-fry on a high heat for an another minute. Add the pepper and continue stir-frying for an additional 2 minutes or so.

3. Stir in the lime leaves, soy sauces and sugar. Add the noodles and tomato, and toss well to heat thoroughly.

4. Sprinkle with chopped basil and serve hot.

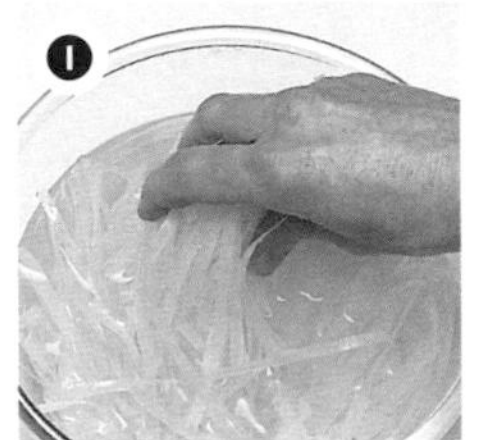

Mumbar

INGREDIENTS

BAHARAT SEASONING MIX
2 tbsp black peppercorns
1 tbsp coriander seeds
2 tsp whole cloves
1½ tsp cumin seeds
1 tsp cardamom seeds
1 cinnamon stick, broken into small pieces
1 whole nutmeg
2 tbsp hot paprika

100 g/3½ oz basmati rice
900 g/2 lb ground lamb
1 small onion, chopped finely
3–4 garlic cloves, crushed
1 bunch each flat-leaved parsley and coriander, chopped finely
2–3 tbsp tomato ketchup
1 tbsp vegetable oil
pared rind and juice of 1 lime
850 ml/1½ pints hot lamb stock
salt and pepper

easy

serves 6–8

30 minutes

25 minutes

❶ To make the baharat seasoning, grind the first 6 ingredients into a fine powder. Grate the whole nutmeg into the mix and stir in the paprika. Store in an airtight jar.

❷ Bring a pan of salted water to the boil. Pour in the rice, return to the boil, and simmer until the rice is tender, but firm to the bite. Drain and rinse.

❸ Place the lamb in a large bowl and break up with a fork. Add the onion, garlic, parsley, coriander, ketchup and 1 teaspoon of the baharat. Stir in the cooked rice, and season. Squeeze the mixture to make it paste-like.

❹ Divide into 4–6 pieces and roll each into a sausage 2.5 cm/1 inch thick. Brush a 23–25 cm/9–10 inch frying pan with the oil. Starting in the centre of the pan, coil the sausage pieces, joining them to form one long sausage.

❺ Press lightly to make an even layer, then tuck the lime rind between the spaces in the sausage. Pour the lime juice and hot stock into the pan and cover with a heatproof plate.

❻ Bring to the boil, then simmer gently for 10 minutes. Cover, continue to cook for 15 minutes, and remove from the heat. Drain, and slide the sausage onto a serving plate. Sprinkle with a pinch of baharat to serve.

Red Pork Curry with Jasmine-scented Rice

INGREDIENTS

RED CURRY PASTE
1 tbsp coriander seeds
2 tsp cumin seeds
2 tsp black or white peppercorns
1 tsp salt, or to taste
5–8 dried red chillies
3–4 shallots, chopped
6–8 garlic cloves
5 cm/2 inch piece fresh ginger, chopped
2 tsp kaffir lime rind
1 tbsp red chilli powder
1 tbsp shrimp paste
2 stalks lemon grass, thinly sliced

900 g/2 lb boned pork shoulder, cut into thin slices
850 ml/1½ pints coconut milk
2 fresh red chillies, deseeded and sliced
2 tbsp Thai fish sauce
2 tsp brown sugar
1 large red pepper, deseeded and sliced
6 kaffir lime leaves
½ bunch fresh mint
½ bunch Thai basil
jasmine-scented or Thai fragrant rice, to serve

easy

serves 4–6

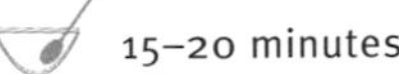
15–20 minutes

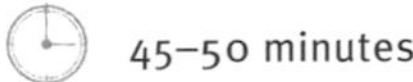
45–50 minutes

❶ To make the red curry paste, grind the coriander seeds, cumin seeds, peppercorns and salt to a fine powder. Add the chillies, one by one, according to taste, and grind in.

❷ Put the shallots, garlic, ginger, kaffir lime rind, chilli powder and shrimp paste in a food processor. Process for 1 minute. Add the ground spices and process again. Adding water, a few drops at a time, continue to process until a thick paste forms. Put in a bowl and stir in the lemon grass.

❸ Put about half the red curry paste with the pork in a large, deep, heavy-based frying pan. Cook over a medium heat for 2–3 minutes, stirring gently, until the pork is evenly coated and begins to brown.

❹ Stir in the coconut milk and bring to the boil. Cook, stirring frequently, for about 10 minutes. Reduce the heat, stir in the chillies, Thai fish sauce and brown sugar, and simmer for about 20 minutes. Add the red pepper and simmer for another 10 minutes.

❺ Shred the lime leaves, mint and basil. Add the lime leaves and half the mint and basil to the curry. Transfer to a serving dish, sprinkle with the remaining mint and basil, and serve with the Thai fragrant rice.

❸

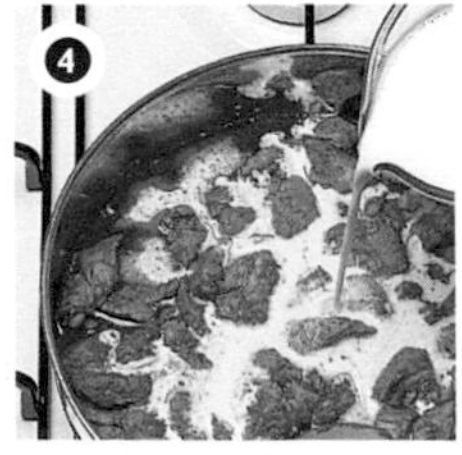
❹

Fish & Seafood

Some people love the taste of ultra-fresh fish and seafood. Others make it a regular part of their diet because it is first-class low-fat, high-protein food. Whichever type you are, you will find recipes in these pages to enhance your enjoyment of fish and crustaceans from river and sea. Spicy flavourings and fast sizzling will transform them. Fish Tacos are made from white fish sprinkled with spices, fried until golden, and served in a soft corn tortilla, accompanied by a crisp cabbage salad. And Moroccan Fish Tagine partners red mullet with a spicy tomato sauce.

Steamed Yellow Fish

INGREDIENTS

500 g/1 lb 2 oz firm fish fillets, such as red snapper or sole
1 dried red bird's-eye chilli
1 small onion, chopped
3 garlic cloves, chopped
2 sprigs fresh coriander
1 tsp coriander seeds
½ tsp turmeric
½ tsp ground black pepper
1 tbsp Thai fish sauce
2 tbsp coconut milk
1 small egg, beaten
2 tbsp rice flour

TO SERVE
soy sauce
stir-fried vegetables
salad

 very easy

 serves 4

 20 minutes

 15–20 minutes

COOK'S TIP
If you do not have a steamer, improvise by placing a large metal colander over a large pan of boiling water. Cover it with an upturned plate to enclose the fish as it steams.

❶ Remove any skin from the fish and cut the fillets diagonally into long, 2 cm/¾ inch wide strips.

❷ Place the dried chilli, onion, garlic, coriander and coriander seeds in a mortar, and grind them with a pestle to a smooth paste.

❸ Add the turmeric, pepper, fish sauce, coconut milk and beaten egg, stirring well to mix evenly.

❹ Dip the fish strips into the paste mixture, then into the rice flour to coat them lightly.

❺ Bring the water in the bottom of a steamer to a boil, then arrange the fish strips in the top of the steamer. Cover, and steam for 12–15 minutes until the fish is just firm.

❻ Serve the fish with soy sauce and an accompaniment of stir-fried vegetables or salad.

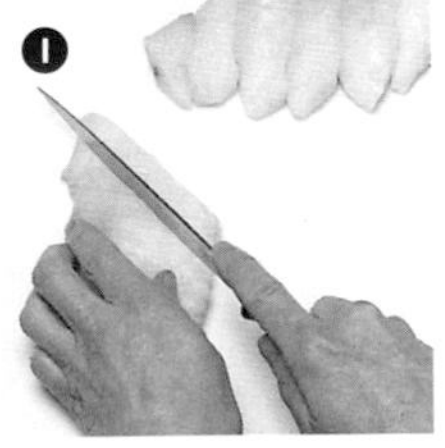

Baked Fish with Peppers, Chillies & Basil

INGREDIENTS

handful of fresh basil leaves
2 tbsp groundnut oil
750 g/1 lb 10 oz whole red snapper, sea bass or John Dory, cleaned
2 tbsp Thai fish sauce
2 garlic cloves, crushed
1 tsp galangal or ginger, grated finely
2 large fresh red chillies, sliced diagonally
1 yellow pepper, deseeded and diced
1 tbsp palm sugar (or brown sugar)
1 tbsp rice vinegar
2 tbsp water or fish stock
2 tomatoes, deseeded and sliced into thin wedges

 very easy

 serves 4

 25 minutes

 35–40 minutes

COOK'S TIP
Large red chillies are not as hot as tiny bird's-eye chillies, so you can use them more freely in dishes which require a mild spiciness.

1. Reserve a few fresh basil leaves for garnish and tuck the rest inside the body cavity of the fish.

2. Heat 1 tablespoon of the oil in a wide frying pan and fry the fish quickly, turning once, until browned. Place the fish on a large piece of foil in a roasting tin and spoon the fish sauce over it. Wrap loosely with foil and bake in an oven preheated to 190°C/375°F/Gas Mark 5 for 25–30 minutes until just cooked through.

3. Meanwhile, heat the remaining oil and fry the garlic, galangal and chillies for 30 seconds. Add the pepper and stir-fry for an additional 2–3 minutes to soften.

4. Stir in the sugar, rice vinegar and water, then add the tomatoes and bring to the boil. Remove from the heat.

5. Take the fish out of the oven and transfer to a warmed serving plate. Add the fish juices to the tin, then spoon the sauce over the fish and scatter with the reserved basil leaves. Serve immediately.

1

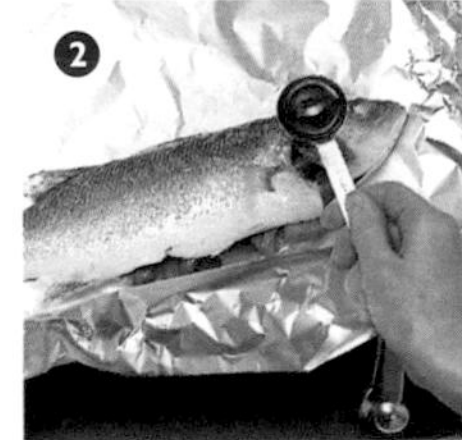
2

Thai-spiced Salmon

INGREDIENTS

SPICE MIXTURE
2.5 cm/1 inch piece fresh root ginger, grated
1 tsp coriander seeds, crushed
¼ tsp chilli powder
1 tbsp lime juice
1 tsp sesame oil

4 pieces salmon fillet with skin, about 150 g/5¼ oz each
2 tbsp vegetable oil

 very easy

 serves 4

 5 minutes, plus 30 minutes to chill

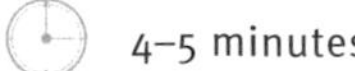 4–5 minutes

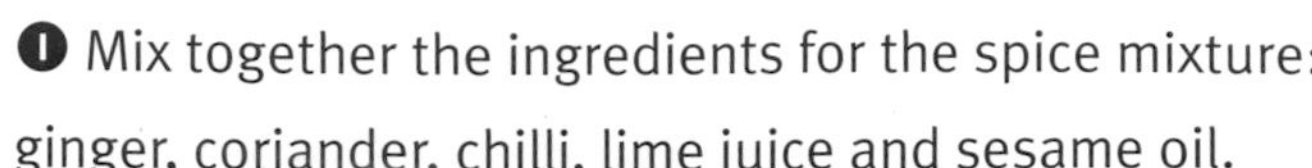

1. Mix together the ingredients for the spice mixture: ginger, coriander, chilli, lime juice and sesame oil.

2. Place the salmon in a wide, non-metal dish and spoon the spice mixture over the flesh side of the fillets, spreading it to coat each piece of salmon evenly.

3. Cover the dish with clingfilm and chill the salmon in the refrigerator for 30 minutes.

4. Heat the vegetable oil in a wide, heavy-based frying pan over a high heat. Place the salmon in it, skin side down.

5. Cook the salmon for 4–5 minutes, without turning (see Cook's Tip), until it is crusty underneath and the flesh flakes easily. Serve immediately.

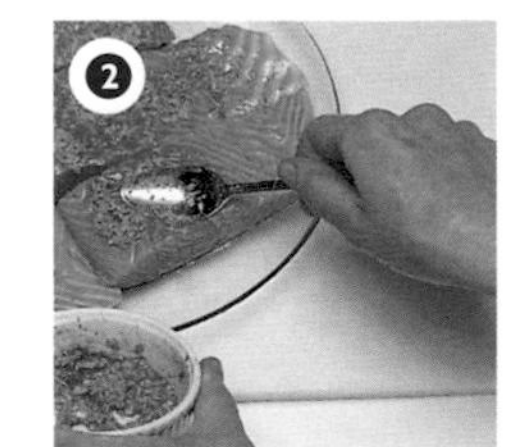

COOK'S TIP
It is important to use a heavy-based pan for this recipe so that the fish cooks evenly without sticking. If the fish is very thick, you may need to turn it over carefully and cook it on the other side for 2–3 minutes.

Spicy Scallops with Lime & Chilli

INGREDIENTS

16 large scallops
1 tbsp butter
1 tbsp vegetable oil
1 tsp crushed garlic
1 tsp grated fresh ginger
1 bunch spring onions, finely sliced
finely grated rind of 1 kaffir lime
1 small red chilli, deseeded and sliced
3 tbsp kaffir lime juice
salt and pepper

TO SERVE
lime wedges
boiled rice

very easy

serves 4

10 minutes

7–8 minutes

COOK'S TIP
If fresh scallops are not available, use frozen ones, but thaw them thoroughly before you cook them. Drain off all excess moisture, and pat them dry with kitchen paper.

1. Trim the scallops to remove any black intestine, then wash and pat dry with kitchen paper. Separate the corals from the white parts, then slice each white part in half horizontally, making 2 rounds.

2. Heat the butter and oil in a wok. Add the garlic and ginger, and stir-fry for 1 minute, without browning. Add the spring onions and stir-fry for 1 more minute.

3. Add the scallops and continue stir-frying over a high heat for 4–5 minutes. Stir in the lime rind, chilli and lime juice, and cook for another minute.

4. Serve the scallops hot, with the juices spooned over them, accompanied by lime wedges and boiled rice.

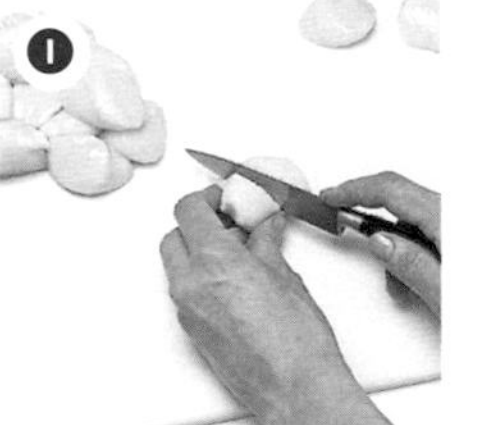

Fish Tacos

INGREDIENTS

450 g/1 lb firm-fleshed white fish, such as red snapper or cod
¼ tsp dried oregano
¼ tsp ground cumin
1 tsp mild chilli powder
2–3 garlic cloves, finely chopped
salt and pepper
3 tbsp plain flour
vegetable oil, for frying

CABBAGE SALAD
¼ red cabbage, thinly sliced or shredded
juice of 2 limes
hot pepper sauce or salsa to taste

TO FINISH
8 soft corn tortillas
1 tbsp chopped fresh coriander
½ onion, chopped (optional)
salsa of your choice

easy

serves 4

15 minutes

20 minutes

1. Place the fish on a plate and sprinkle with half the oregano, cumin, chilli powder and garlic. Season with salt and pepper, then dust with the flour.

2. Heat the oil in a frying pan until it is smoking, then fry the fish in several batches until it is golden on the outside, and just tender in the middle. Remove from the pan and place on kitchen paper to drain.

3. To make the cabbage salad, combine the cabbage with the remaining oregano, cumin, chilli and garlic. Stir in the lime juice, and add salt and hot pepper sauce to taste.

4. Warm the tortillas, one by one, in an ungreased non-stick frying pan, sprinkling with a few drops of water as they heat. As you work, wrap the tortillas in a clean tea towel to keep them warm. Another method is to heat a stack of tortillas in the pan, alternating the top and bottom tortillas so that they warm evenly.

5. Place some of the warm fried fish in each tortilla, with a big spoonful of the cabbage salad. Sprinkle with fresh coriander and onion, if desired. Add salsa to taste and serve the tacos at once.

2

3

5

Thai Crab Omelette

INGREDIENTS

225 g/8 oz white crab meat, fresh or thawed if frozen
3 spring onions, finely chopped
1 tbsp chopped coriander
1 tbsp chopped chives
pinch cayenne pepper
2 tbsp vegetable oil
2 garlic cloves, crushed
1 tsp freshly grated ginger root
1 red chilli, deseeded and finely chopped
2 tbsp lime juice
2 lime leaves, shredded
2 tsp sugar
2 tsp Thai fish sauce
3 eggs
4 tbsp coconut cream
1 tsp salt
spring onion slivers, to garnish

easy

serves 4

10 minutes, plus 2–3 hours to chill

15 minutes

COOK'S TIP
You can also serve this omelette warm. After adding the crab, cook for 3–4 minutes to heat through, then serve immediately.

❶ Put the crab meat into a bowl and check there are no small pieces of shell in it. Add the spring onions, coriander, chives and cayenne, and set aside.

❷ Heat 1 tablespoon of vegetable oil and add the garlic, ginger and chilli, and stir-fry for 30 seconds. Add the lime juice, lime leaves, sugar and fish sauce. Simmer the mixture for 3–4 minutes until reduced. Remove from the heat and allow to cool. Add to the crab mixture and set aside.

❸ Beat the eggs with the coconut cream and salt. In a frying pan, heat the remaining vegetable oil over a medium heat. Add the egg mixture and, as it sets on the bottom, pull the edges toward the centre, so unset egg runs underneath.

❹ When the omelette is nearly set, spoon the crab mixture down the centre of it. Cook for an additional 1–2 minutes to finish cooking the egg, then turn the omelette out of the pan onto a serving dish. Allow to cool, then refrigerate for 2–3 hours or overnight. To serve, cut into 4 pieces and garnish with slivers of spring onion.

Moroccan Fish Tagine

INGREDIENTS

2 tbsp olive oil
1 large onion, finely chopped
large pinch saffron
½ tsp ground cinnamon
1 tsp ground coriander
½ tsp ground cumin
½ tsp ground turmeric
200 g/7 oz canned chopped tomatoes
375 ml/13 fl oz fish stock
4 small red mullet, cleaned and boned, minus heads and tails
85 g/3 oz pitted green olives
1 tbsp chopped preserved lemon
3 tbsp fresh chopped coriander
salt and pepper
couscous, to serve

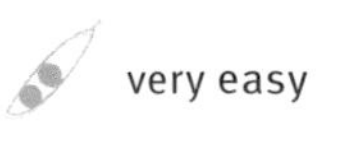
very easy

serves 4

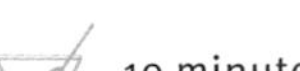
10 minutes

1 hour 15 minutes

PRESERVED LEMON
Quarter the fruit lengthways (do not cut right through). Pack in a jar with 35 g/1/4 oz sea salt per lemon. Add the juice of a lemon and top up with water. Leave for at least 1 month.

❶ Heat the olive oil in a large saucepan or flameproof casserole. Add the onion and cook gently for 10 minutes, without allowing it to colour, until softened. Add the saffron, cinnamon, ground coriander, cumin and turmeric, and cook for an additional 30 seconds, stirring.

❷ Add the chopped tomatoes and fish stock and stir well. Bring to the boil, cover, and simmer for 15 minutes. Uncover and simmer for an additional 20–35 minutes until the sauce has thickened.

❸ Cut each red mullet in half, then add the pieces to the pan, pushing them into the sauce. Simmer gently for an additional 5–6 minutes until the fish is just cooked.

❹ Carefully stir in the olives and preserved lemon, and the chopped fresh coriander. Season and serve with couscous.

Curried Tiger Prawns with Courgettes

INGREDIENTS

350 g/12 oz small courgettes
1 tsp salt
450 g/1 lb cooked tiger prawns
5 tbsp vegetable oil
4 garlic cloves, finely chopped
5 tbsp chopped coriander
1 fresh green chilli, deseeded, chopped
½ tsp ground turmeric
1½ tsp ground cumin
pinch cayenne pepper
200 g/7 oz canned chopped tomatoes
1 tsp freshly grated ginger
1 tbsp lemon juice
steamed basmati rice, to serve

 very easy

 serves 4

 40 minutes

 15–20 minutes

COOK'S TIP
You can use smaller cooked prawns instead of tiger prawns, but these release quite a lot of liquid, so you may need to increase the simmering time to thicken the sauce.

❶ Wash and trim the courgettes. Cut into small batons. Put into a colander and sprinkle with a little of the salt. Set aside for 30 minutes. Rinse, drain, and pat dry. Spread the prawns on kitchen paper to drain.

❷ In a wok or a frying pan, heat the oil over a high heat. Add the garlic and as soon as it begins to brown, add the courgettes, coriander, green chilli, turmeric, cumin, cayenne, tomatoes, ginger, lemon juice and remaining salt. Stir well and bring to the boil.

❸ Cover and simmer over a low heat for about 5 minutes. Uncover and add the prawns.

❹ Increase the heat to high and simmer the curry for about 5 minutes to reduce the liquid to a thick sauce. Serve immediately, accompanied by steamed basmati rice and garnished with lime wedges.

Vegetables & Side Dishes

Exciting main dishes may be served with plain boiled rice or vegetables, yet side dishes and salads need to complement a main dish in interesting ways. As the following pages show, if prepared with a few extra ingredients they may take on new life. For example, horseradish brings a kick to a Red Rice Salad with Hot Dressing, while a cool Thai Green Salad is enlivened with thin cucumber slices and toasted coconut. Pickles are an essential accompaniment to Eastern dishes, bringing contrasting textures and tastes, and here you will find a recipe for Crisp Pickled Vegetables.

Crisp Pickled Vegetables

INGREDIENTS

½ small cauliflower
½ cucumber
2 medium carrots
200 g/7 oz green beans
½ small Chinese cabbage
700 ml/1¼ pints rice vinegar
1 tbsp sugar
1 tsp salt

SPICE PASTE
3 garlic cloves
3 shallots
3 red bird's-eye chillies
5 tbsp groundnut oil

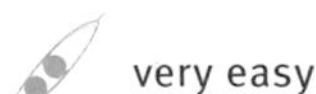

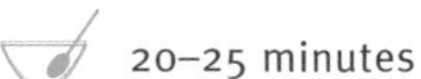

very easy

serves 6–8

20–25 minutes

15 minutes

COOK'S TIP

To make simple carrot flowers, peel a carrot thinly, then use a small, sharp knife to cut narrow channels down the length of it at regular intervals. Slice the carrot in the usual way and the slices will resemble flowers.

1. Trim the cauliflower. Peel and deseed the cucumber. Peel the carrots. Top and tail the beans. Trim the cabbage. Cut all the vegetables into bite-sized pieces. If you have time, cut the carrots into flower shapes (see Cook's Tip).

2. Place the rice vinegar, sugar and salt in a large pan and bring almost to a boil. Add the vegetables, lower the heat, and simmer for 3–4 minutes until they are just tender, but still crisp inside. Remove the pan from the heat and leave the vegetables and vinegar to cool.

3. To make the spice paste, peel the garlic and shallots and deseed the chillies. Place them all in a mortar and grind with a pestle until a smooth paste forms.

4. Heat the oil in a wok and stir-fry the spice paste gently for 1–2 minutes. Add the vegetables and the vinegar, and cook for an additional 2 minutes to reduce the liquid slightly. Remove from the heat and leave to cool.

5. Serve the pickles cold, or pack them into jars and store them in the refrigerator for up to 2 weeks.

1

3

4

Chilli & Coconut Sambal

INGREDIENTS

1 small coconut
1 slice fresh pineapple, diced finely
1 small onion, chopped finely
2 small green chillies, deseeded and chopped
5 cm/2 inch piece lemon grass
½ tsp salt
1 tsp shrimp paste
1 tbsp lime juice
2 tbsp chopped fresh coriander
coriander sprigs, to garnish

 extremely easy

 serves 6–8

 15–20 minutes

 0 minutes

❶ Puncture 2 of the coconut eyes with a screwdriver and pour the milk out from the shell. Crack the shell, prise away the flesh, and grate it coarsely into a bowl.

❷ Mix the coconut with the pineapple, onion, chillies and lemon grass.

❸ Blend together the salt, shrimp paste and lime juice, then stir into the sambal.

❹ Stir in the coriander. Spoon into a small dish to serve.

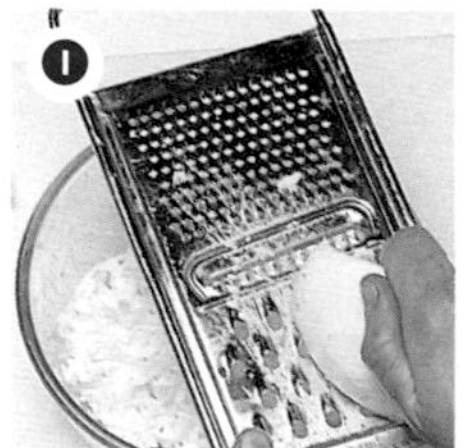

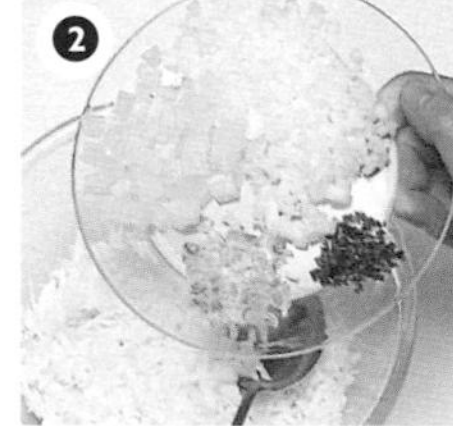

COOK'S TIP
Grate the coconut quickly by using a grating blade on a food processor.

Thai Bean Curry

INGREDIENTS

400 g/14 oz green beans, topped and tailed
1 garlic clove, sliced finely
1 red bird's-eye chilli, deseeded and chopped
½ tsp paprika pepper
1 piece lemon grass stalk, chopped finely
2 tsp Thai fish sauce
125 ml/4 fl oz coconut milk
1 tbsp sunflower oil
2 spring onions, sliced

1. Cut the beans into 5 cm/2 inch pieces and cook in boiling water for 2 minutes. Drain well.
2. Place the garlic, chilli, paprika, lemon grass, fish sauce and coconut milk in a blender, and process until they form a smooth paste.
3. Heat the oil and stir-fry the spring onions over a high heat for about 1 minute. Add the paste and bring the mixture to the boil.
4. Simmer for 3–4 minutes to reduce the liquid by about half. Add the beans and simmer the curry for an additional 1–2 minutes until tender. Serve hot.

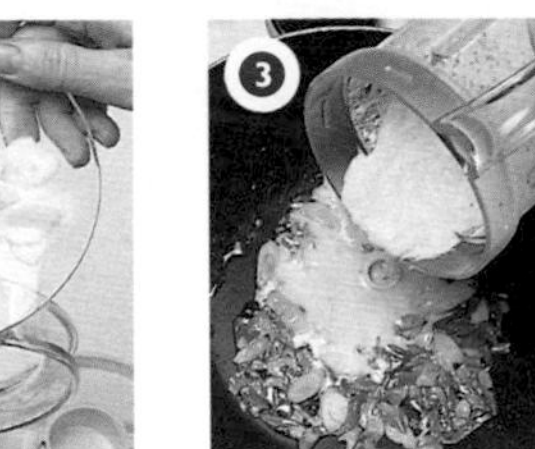

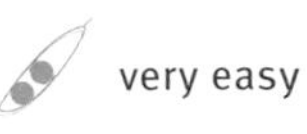
very easy

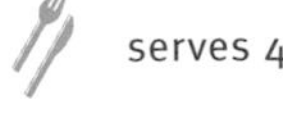
serves 4

15 minutes

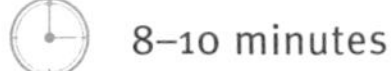
8–10 minutes

COOK'S TIP
Young runner beans may be used instead of green beans. Remove strings from the beans, then cut on the diagonal into short pieces. Cook as above until tender.

Potatoes in Creamed Coconut

INGREDIENTS

600 g/1 lb 5 oz potatoes
1 onion, sliced thinly
2 red bird's-eye chillies, chopped
½ tsp salt
½ tsp ground black pepper
125 ml/4 fl oz creamed coconut
450 ml/16 fl oz vegetable or chicken stock
chopped fresh coriander or basil, to garnish

❶ Peel the potatoes thinly and cut into 2 cm/¾ inch chunks.

❷ Place the potatoes in a pan with the onion, chilli, salt, pepper and creamed coconut. Stir in the stock.

❸ Bring the mixture to the boil, stirring, then lower the heat and cover the pan. Simmer gently, stirring occasionally, until the potatoes are tender.

❹ Adjust the seasoning to taste, then sprinkle with chopped coriander or basil. Serve hot.

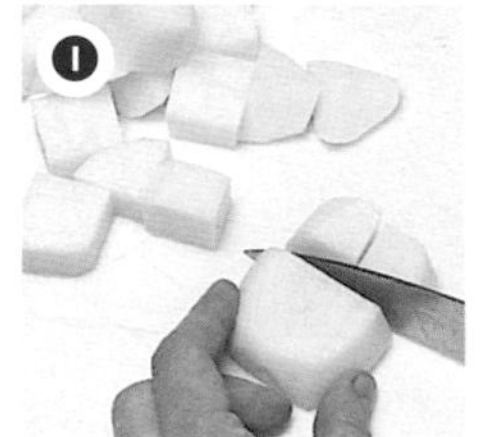

 very easy

 serves 4

 10 minutes

 15–20 minutes

COOK'S TIP

If the potatoes are a thin-skinned or new variety, wash or scrub them to remove any dirt, and cook them with the skins on. This adds extra dietary fibre and nutrients to the finished dish, and cuts preparation time.

Thai Green Salad

INGREDIENTS

1 small head Cos lettuce
1 bunch spring onions
½ cucumber
4 tbsp coarsely shredded fresh coconut, toasted

DRESSING
4 tbsp lime juice
2 tbsp Thai fish sauce
1 small bird's-eye chilli, chopped finely
1 tsp sugar
1 garlic clove, crushed
2 tbsp chopped fresh coriander
1 tbsp chopped fresh mint

 extremely easy

 serves 4–6

 15 minutes

 0 minutes

COOK'S TIP
This salad is good for picnics. Pack the leaves into a large plastic container, then nestle the screw-top jar of dressing in the centre. Cover with a lid or with clingfilm. Packed this way, the salad stays crisp. If the dressing leaks, there is no mess.

1. Tear or roughly shred the lettuce leaves and place them in a large salad bowl.

2. Trim and thinly slice the spring onions diagonally, and add to the salad bowl.

3. Use a vegetable peeler to shave thin slices from along the length of the cucumber and add these to the bowl.

4. Place all the ingredients for the dressing in a screw-top jar and shake well to mix thoroughly.

5. Pour the dressing over the salad and toss well to coat the leaves evenly. Scatter the coconut over the salad and toss in lightly just before serving.

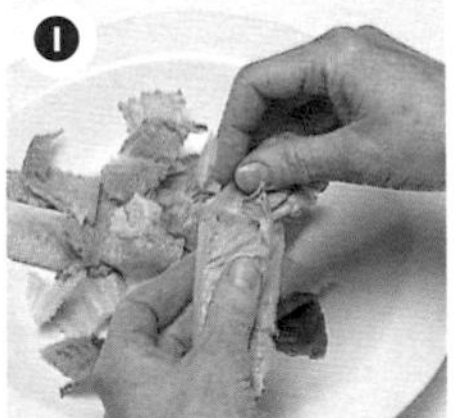

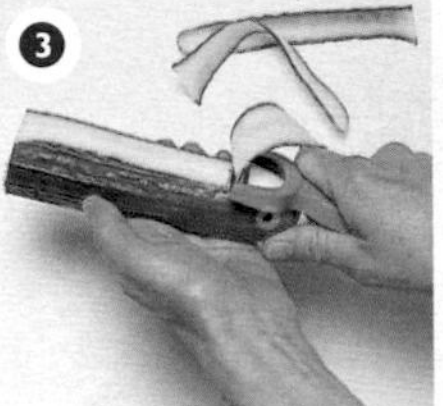

Red Rice Salad with Hot Dressing

INGREDIENTS

1 tbsp olive oil
200 g/7 oz red rice
700 ml/1¼ pints water
400 g/14 oz canned red kidney beans, rinsed and drained
1 small red pepper, deseeded and diced
1 small red onion, chopped finely
2 small cooked beetroot (not in vinegar), peeled and diced
6–8 radishes, sliced thinly
2–3 tbsp chopped fresh chives
salt and pepper
fresh chives, to garnish

HOT DRESSING
2 tbsp prepared horseradish
1 tbsp Dijon mustard
1 tsp sugar
50 ml/2 fl oz red wine vinegar
125 ml/4 fl oz extra-virgin olive oil

 very easy

 serves 6–8

 15–20 minutes, plus 1 hour to stand

 20 minutes

COOK'S TIP
The cooking time for red rice varies according to the variety.

1. Put the olive oil and red rice in a heavy-based saucepan and place over medium heat. Add the water and 1 teaspoon of salt. Bring to the boil, reduce the heat and simmer, covered, until the rice is tender and all the water is absorbed (see Cook's Tip). Remove from the heat and allow the rice to cool to room temperature.

2. To make the hot dressing, put the horseradish, mustard and sugar in a small bowl and whisk to combine. Then gradually whisk in the vinegar, followed by the oil, to form a smooth dressing.

3. In a large bowl, combine the red kidney beans, red pepper, red onion, beetroot, radishes and chives, and toss together. Season with salt and pepper.

4. Using a fork, fluff the rice into the bowl with the vegetables and toss. Pour the dressing over it and toss well. Cover and let the salad stand for about 1 hour. Spoon into a large, shallow serving bowl, garnish with fresh chives, and serve immediately.

Chinese Fried Rice

INGREDIENTS

2–3 tbsp groundnut or vegetable oil
2 onions, halved and cut lengthways into thin wedges
2 garlic cloves, thinly sliced
2.5 cm/1 inch piece fresh ginger root, peeled, sliced, and cut into slivers
200 g/7 oz cooked ham, thinly sliced
700 g/1lb 9 oz cold, cooked long-grain white rice
250 g/9 oz cooked peeled prawns
115 g/4 oz canned water chestnuts, sliced
3 eggs
3 tsp sesame oil
4–6 spring onions, diagonally sliced into 2.5 cm/1 inch pieces
2 tbsp dark soy sauce or Thai fish sauce
1 tbsp sweet chilli sauce
2 tbsp chopped fresh coriander or flat-leaved parsley
salt and pepper

 easy

 serves 4–6

 15–20 minutes

 10–15 minutes

❶ Heat 2–3 tablespoons groundnut oil in a wok or large, deep frying pan, until very hot. Add the onions and stir-fry for about 2 minutes until they begin to soften. Add the garlic and ginger, and stir-fry for another minute. Add the ham strips and stir to combine.

❷ Stir the cold cooked rice into the vegetables and ham mixture, then add the prawns and water chestnuts. Stir in 2 tablespoons of water and quickly cover the pan. Continue to cook for 2 minutes, shaking the pan occasionally to prevent sticking and to allow the rice to heat through.

❸ Beat the eggs with 1 teaspoon of the sesame oil, and season with salt and pepper. Make a well in the centre of the rice mixture and add the eggs. Stir immediately, gradually drawing the rice into the eggs.

❹ Stir in the spring onions, soy and chilli sauces and stir-fry. Stir in a little more water if the rice looks dry or is sticking. Drizzle in the remaining sesame oil and stir. Season to taste with salt and pepper.

❺ Remove from the heat, wipe the edge of the pan and sprinkle the coriander over the fried rice. Serve immediately, straight from the pan.

Singapore Noodles

INGREDIENTS

55 g/2 oz dried Chinese mushrooms
225 g/8 oz rice noodles
2–3 tbsp groundnut oil
6–8 garlic cloves, sliced
2–3 shallots, sliced
2.5 cm/1 inch fresh ginger root, peeled and sliced
4–5 fresh red chillies, deseeded and sliced
225 g/8 oz chicken breast meat, sliced
225 g/8 oz mangetouts, sliced diagonally
225 g/8 oz Chinese leaves, shredded
225 g/8 oz cooked peeled prawns
6–8 water chestnuts
2 spring onions, sliced
2 tbsp chopped fresh coriander or mint

CURRY SAUCE
2 tbsp rice wine or dry sherry
2 tbsp soy sauce
3 tbsp medium or hot Madras curry powder
1 tbsp sugar
550 ml/19 fl oz canned coconut milk
salt and black pepper

very easy

serves 4–6

20 minutes, plus 15 minutes to soak

9–10 minutes

❶ To make the curry sauce, whisk the rice wine and soy sauce into the curry powder, then stir in the remaining ingredients (sugar, coconut milk and seasoning).

❷ Put the Chinese mushrooms in a small bowl and add enough boiling water to cover them. Soak them for about 15 minutes until softened. Lift out and squeeze out the liquid. Discard any stems, then slice thinly and set aside. Soak the rice noodles according to the instructions on the package, then drain well.

❸ Heat the oil in a wok or a deep frying pan over a medium-high heat. Add the garlic, shallots, ginger and chillies, and stir-fry for about 30 seconds. Add the chicken strips and the mangetouts, and stir-fry for about 2 minutes. Add the Chinese leaves, prawns, water chestnuts, mushrooms and spring onions, and stir-fry for 1–2 minutes. Add the curry sauce and noodles to the pan and stir-fry for 5 minutes. Sprinkle with the fresh coriander, and serve.

Desserts

To finish off your hot and spicy lunch or dinner with a sizzling dessert, this section gives a few ideas. Cool, exotic fruits taste cooler and jazzier when prepared with fresh ginger or dressed with a cardamom-flavoured syrup. Lychee & Ginger Sorbet looks wonderful topped with slices of starfruit and slivers of preserved ginger, while the light and delicious Steamed Coconut Cake with Lime & Ginger makes a perfect end to a Thai-style feast.

Exotic Fruit Salad

INGREDIENTS

1 tsp jasmine tea
1 tsp grated fresh ginger root
1 strip lime rind
125 ml/4 fl oz boiling water
2 tbsp caster sugar
1 papaya
1 mango
½ small pineapple
1 starfruit
2 passion fruits

 extremely easy

 serves 6

 30 minutes, plus 1 hour to chill

 0 minutes

COOK'S TIP
Starfruit have little flavour when unripe, but once ripened and turning yellow, they become delicately sweet and fragrant. Usually by this stage, the tips of the ridges have become brown, so these must be removed before slicing. Run a vegetable peeler along each ridge to do so.

❶ Place the tea, ginger and lime rind in a heatproof cup, and pour the boiling water over them. Leave to infuse for 5 minutes, then strain the liquid.

❷ Add the sugar to the liquid and stir well to dissolve. Leave the resulting syrup until it is completely cool.

❸ Halve, deseed and peel the papaya. Halve the mango, remove its stone, and peel the fruit. Peel the pineapple and remove its core. Cut all the fruit into bite-sized pieces.

❹ Slice the starfruit crossways. Place all the prepared fruit in a wide serving bowl and pour the cooled syrup over them. Cover with clingfilm and chill for about 1 hour.

❺ Cut the passion fruit in half, scoop out the flesh, and mix it with the lime juice. Spoon this over the salad, and serve.

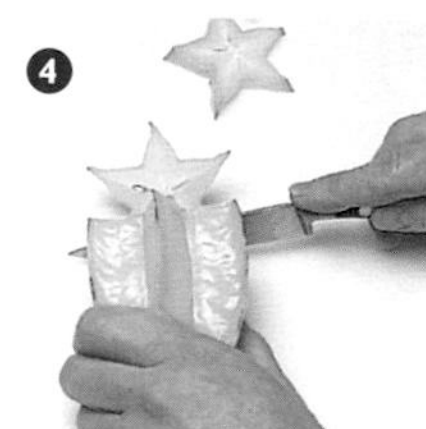

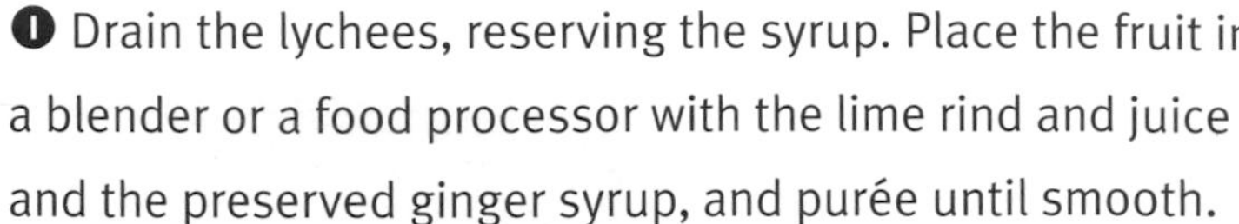

Lychee & Ginger Sorbet

INGREDIENTS

400 g/14 oz canned lychees in syrup
finely grated rind of 1 lime
2 tbsp lime juice
3 tbsp syrup from bottle of preserved ginger
2 egg whites

TO DECORATE
starfruit slices
slivers of preserved ginger

very easy

serves 4

15–20 minutes, plus 2–2½ hours to freeze

0 minutes

COOK'S TIP
It is recommended that raw egg whites are not served to very young children, pregnant women, the elderly or anyone weakened by illness. The egg whites may be left out of this recipe, but to obtain a light texture, the sorbet needs to be whisked a second time after another hour of freezing.

❶ Drain the lychees, reserving the syrup. Place the fruit in a blender or a food processor with the lime rind and juice and the preserved ginger syrup, and purée until smooth.

❷ Mix the purée thoroughly with the reserved lychee syrup and pour the mixture into a freezerproof container. Freeze for 1–1½ hours until slushy in texture. (Alternatively, you can use an ice-cream maker.)

❸ Remove from the freezer and whisk to break up the ice crystals. Whisk the egg whites in a clean, dry bowl until stiff, then fold into the iced mixture quickly and lightly.

❹ Return the sorbet to the freezer and freeze until firm. Serve the sorbet in scoops, decorated with slices of starfruit and strips of preserved ginger.

❶

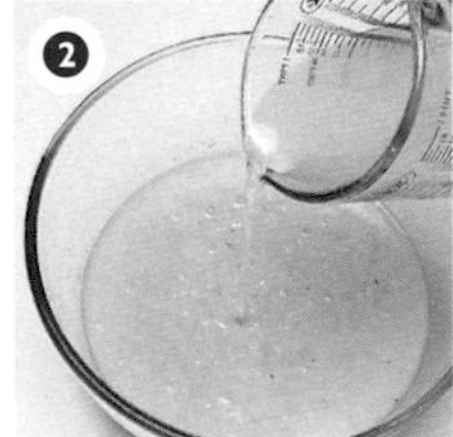
❷

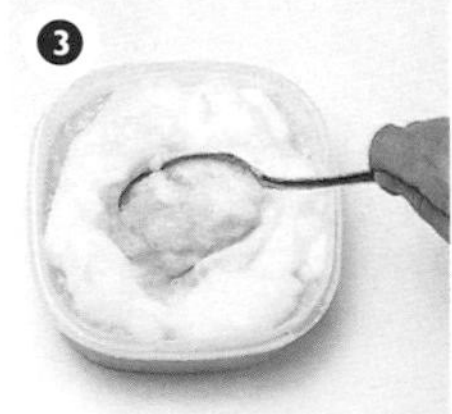
❸

Pineapple with Cardamom & Lime

INGREDIENTS

1 pineapple
2 cardamom pods
1 thinly pared strip lime rind
1 tbsp soft light brown sugar
3 tbsp lime juice

1. Cut the top and base from the pineapple, cut away the peel, and remove the eyes from the flesh. Cut into quarters and remove the core. Slice lengthways (see Cook's Tip).

2. Place the cardamom pods in a mortar and crush with a pestle, then place in a pan with the lime rind and 4 tablespoons water. Heat until boiling, then simmer for 30 seconds. Remove from the heat and add the sugar, then cover and leave to infuse for 5 minutes.

3. Stir in the sugar to dissolve, add the lime juice, then strain the syrup over the pineapple. Chill for 30 minutes.

4. Arrange the pineapple on a serving dish, spoon the syrup over it, and serve.

1

2

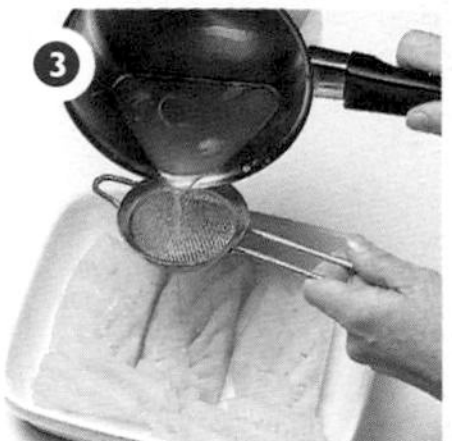
3

easy

serves 4

15 minutes,
plus 35 minutes
to stand & to chill

2–3 minutes

COOK'S TIP

To remove the eyes from pineapple, cut off the peel, then use a sharp knife to cut a V-shaped channel down the pineapple, cutting diagonally through the lines of eyes in the flesh, to make spiralling cuts around the fruit.

Steamed Coconut Cake with Lime & Ginger

INGREDIENTS

2 large eggs, separated
pinch of salt
100 g/3½ oz caster sugar
5 tbsp butter, melted and cooled
5 tbsp coconut milk
150 g/5½ oz self-raising flour
½ tsp baking powder
3 tbsp desiccated coconut
4 tbs stem ginger syrup
3 tbsp lime juice

TO DECORATE
3 pieces stem ginger
curls of grated fresh coconut

❶ Cut an 11 inch round of nonstick paper and press into a 7 inch steamer basket to line it.

❷ Whisk the egg whites with the salt until stiff. Gradually whisk in the sugar 1 tablespoon at a time, whisking hard after each addition until the mixture stands in stiff peaks.

❸ Whisk in the yolks, then quickly stir in the butter and coconut milk. Sift the flour and baking powder over the mixture, then fold in lightly and evenly with a large metal spoon. Fold in the coconut.

❹ Spoon the mixture into the lined steamer basket and tuck the spare paper over the top. Place the basket over boiling water, cover, and steam for 30 minutes.

❺ Turn out the cake onto a plate, remove the paper, and cool slightly. Mix together the ginger and lime juice and spoon over the cake. Cut into squares and decorate with diced, preserved stem ginger and curls of fresh coconut.

 very easy

 serves 8

 15–20 minutes

 30 minutes